I CAN BE AN
ARCHITECT

By Susan Clinton

Prepared under the direction of Robert Hillerich, Ph.D.

℗ CHILDRENS PRESS ®

CHICAGO

Library of Congress Cataloging-in-Publication Data
Clinton, Susan.
  I can be an architect.
  (I can be series)
  Includes index.
  Summary: Briefly describes the work and training of an
architect.
  1. Architecture—Vocational guidance—Juvenile
literature. [1. Architecture—Vocational guidance.
2. Vocational guidance. 3. Occupations] I. Title.
II. Series.
NA1995.C57 1986   720'.23   85-28004
ISBN 0-516-01890-6

PICTURE DICTIONARY

bulldozer

cement mixer

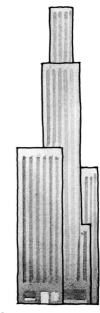

skyscraper

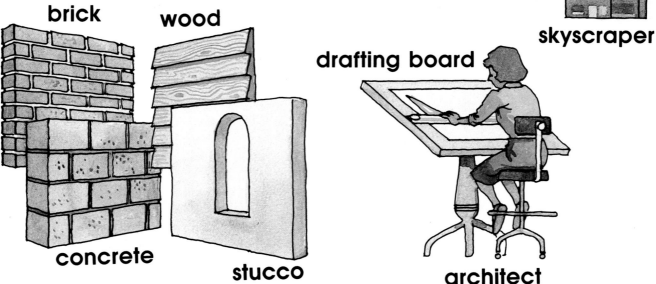

brick

wood

concrete

stucco

drafting board

architect

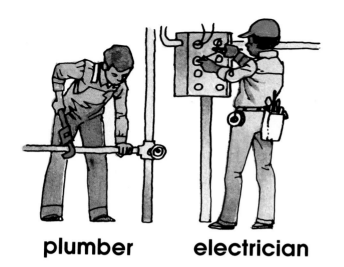

plumber   **electrician**

model

blueprint

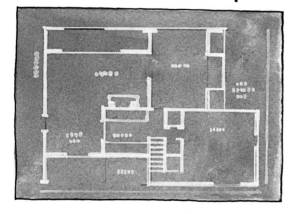

working drawing

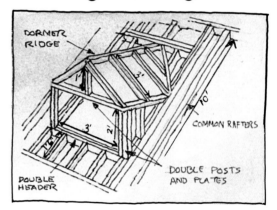

landscaper

Every building was once an idea drawn on paper.

Have you ever watched workers building a house or a store or a skyscraper? How do all the workers know what to do?

skyscraper

architect

They follow very exact plans. Before anyone gets to work putting up a new building with hammers and saws, with bulldozers and cement mixers, an architect gets to work drawing plans.

bulldozer

cement mixer

Architects design
buildings. They also
design other things, such
as parks, airports, and
bridges. While a

building is going up, the
architect often comes to
check on the builder's
work. The architect's job
ends only when the
building is finished.

Construction workers make forms into which concrete will be poured.

The people who hire architects are called clients. An architect's client could be a family that needs to add a new room to its house. A client could be a big company that needs a

Office buildings being built in Dallas, Texas

new office building. Or a client might even be a city that wants to build a new neighborhood with houses, factories, schools, roads, and parks.

Whether the project is large or small, an architect first tries to make a design that is functional—a design that will serve its purpose. But architects also want their buildings to be beautiful. They want people to enjoy using their buildings, or even enjoy just seeing them.

An architect designs a space according to its function.
Above: A suburban home designed by famous architect Frank Lloyd Wright (left).
Oral Roberts University in Tulsa, Oklahoma (right). Below: Nathan Phillips Square
in Toronto, Canada (left). The Illinois State Office Building in Chicago, Illinois (right)

Left: Chicago's John Hancock Center. Right: A Victorian-style house

Think about all the different buildings you see every day. Which ones do you like to see? Which ones do you like to go into?

When architects plan a building, they think

Left: The Flatiron Building in New York City. Right: Marina Towers in Chicago

about how people move
and how people feel
about the spaces
around them. They think
about how much space
people need for different
jobs and activities.

13

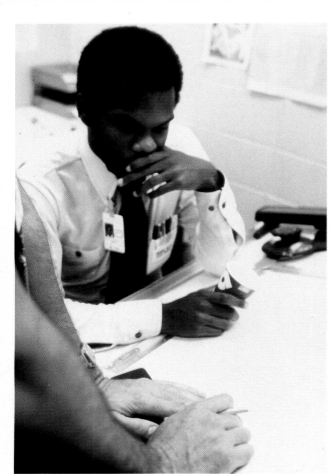

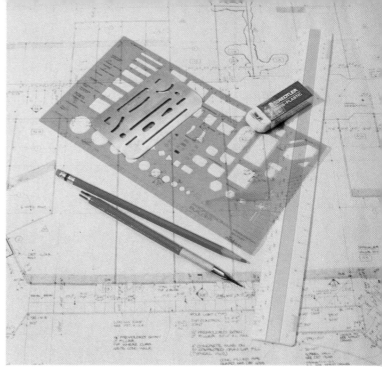

Architects use many drawing tools,
just as builders use building tools.

Architects need to
know how building tools
and materials work and
how much they cost.
They have to be good
at both mathematics
and drawing. They must

14

An architect has much to learn from studying how architects in the past solved building problems.

learn how buildings
were made in the past.
Most importantly,
architects must be able
to put all these things
together to solve
problems.

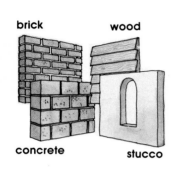

brick   wood

concrete   stucco

How many closets should a house have? Should a building be made of brick, wood, concrete, or stucco? How wide should a school's hall be? What kind of roof is best in very snowy places? Solving problems like these takes training and practice.

An architecture professor goes over his student's drawings.

After high school,
future architects go to
college for five or six
years. Architecture
students spend many
hours in a class called
design studio. Here

An architecture student has a lot to learn. Above: Learning about colors and how to mix them for a model (left). Building a large model (right). Below: Professor gives advice on building a model (left). Working on drawings at home (right)

students work at drafting
boards drawing their
building ideas.

drafting board

Sometimes the teacher
invites judges to choose
the best design.

After they graduate,
the students become
apprentices. An
apprentice works for an
architect for three years
to learn more about the
job.

Architects' drawings even show such details as which way a door opens.

Apprentices may be in
charge of drawing small
details in a building
plan. For example, they
may draw all the
windows or all the bricks
in a building. Sometimes

Architect and assistant study a model of a train station.

they program a
computer to draw these
details. Apprentices also
build small models of
buildings to show clients
exactly how a design
will look.

Finally, every
apprentice must pass a

The moment every student waits for—getting a letter from an architectural firm that will hire him as an apprentice.

state test to earn a license. Passing the test shows that the apprentice's designs will be safe to build and use.

At work, architects talk to many different people. Salesmen come

Left: An architect and his assistant prepare for a client's visit.
Right: Architect and clients on a construction site

to show them new
materials. Clients come
to look at designs and
models. If a client likes
the overall design, the
architect goes on to
draw the final plans, or
blueprints.

It takes a team of architects to design large projects such as office buildings, bridges, and parks.

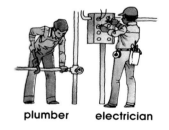

plumber   **electrician**

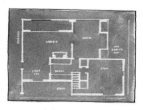

blueprint

Several architects may work together on the blueprints for a large project. Architects talk to plumbers about putting in water pipes. They talk with electricians about wiring lights.

24

Architects check with plumbers and electricians to make sure their drawings will really work. Hard hats must be worn in construction areas to protect people's heads from falling objects.

Above: Working drawings (right) can be very complicated because of all the measurements they show. Architect (left) compares his plans to a project that is almost completed. Below: Architect and builder discuss details of a drawing.

Then the architects
and apprentices make
working drawings from
the blueprints. Working
drawings give
measurements for every
part of the building.

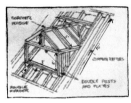

working drawing

Architects talk with
builders to make sure
they follow the working
drawings exactly.

Yards, driveways, sidewalks, and even bushes and trees
are all planned on the drawing board.

landscaper

Landscapers help
architects choose trees
and bushes to plant
around their buildings.
    Finally the architect
can put away all the
drawings and blueprints.

The design has become
a real place for people
to use and enjoy.

WORDS YOU SHOULD KNOW

apprentice (uh • PREN • tiss)—someone who is learning a skill by working for a person who has that skill

architecture (AR • ki • tek • shur)—the art of designing buildings and the spaces around them

blueprints (BLOO • prints)—drawings of the plans for a building, with white lines on a blue background

bulldozer (BULL • doh • zer)—a machine like a tractor, used for clearing land and making roads

cement (sih • MENT)—a grey powder made of many minerals that is used to make concrete

client (KLY • ent)—a person who uses the services of another

concrete (KAHN • kreet)—a building material made of cement mixed with sand, gravel, and water. It is used to make walls and floors

design (dee • ZYN)—to draw a plan for something to be built. The drawing is also called a design.

drafting board (DRAFT • ing BOHRD)—a high, slanted table where an architect makes drawings

electrician (ee • lek • TRIH • shun)—a worker who installs and fixes wires and lights

functional (FUNK • shun • ul)—able to serve a certain purpose

hire (HYR)—to pay someone to do some job or service

landscaper (LAND • skay • per)—a person who designs land for yards, gardens, or parks

measurements (MEH • zhur • ments)—numbers showing how long, wide, or deep an object is

plumber (PLUM • er)—a worker who installs and fixes water pipes

project (PRAH • jekt)—a job, plan, or design

salespeople (SAILZ • peep • il)—people whose job is selling things

skyscraper (SKY • skraip • er)—a very tall building

stucco (STUCK • oh)—a building material like plaster or cement, used for the inside or outside walls of a building

INDEX

PHOTO CREDITS

ABOUT THE AUTHOR

Susan Clinton holds a Ph.D. in English and is a part-time teacher of English Literature at Northwestern University in Chicago. Her articles have appeared in such publications as *Consumer's Digest, Family Style Magazine,* and the Chicago *Reader.* In addition, she has been a contributor to *Encyclopaedia Britannica* and *Compton's Encyclopedia,* and has written reader stories and other materials for a number of educational publishers. Ms. Clinton lives in Chicago and is the mother of two boys.